Rhonda S. Edwards

One Acorn's Journey

The Legend of the Angel Oak

Illustrated by Wendy S. Tyree

One Acorn's Journey
THE LEGEND OF THE ANGEL OAK

iUniverse books may be ordered through booksellers or by contacting:

iUniverse
1663 Liberty Drive
Bloomington, IN 47403
www.iuniverse.com
844-349-9409

ISBN: 978-1-6632-2721-8 (sc)
ISBN: 978-1-6632-2722-5 (e)

Library of Congress Control Number: 2021915722

Print information available on the last page.

iUniverse rev. date: 07/30/2021

One Acorn's Journey

In memory of Flaudia Verecia Harrelson Currie, my great-grandmother.

Special thanks to my sister, the illustrator, for pouring her love of nature into the beauty of her artwork. I feel she makes the story of the Angel Oak's life come alive.

Preface

The idea for the book, *One Acorn's Journey: The Legend of the Angel Oak*, was born after visiting the Angel Oak with my family. The amazement and wonder we experienced as we walked around, underneath, and among the winding branches that disappeared underground in many places made me realize that those who will never see this historic tree will miss those emotions. To ensure that others learn of this live oak tree's journey, I decided to do some research and began writing the legend of the Angel Oak. As my research progressed, I came to learn that this tree was in danger of being cut down to make room for housing. The fear of this actually happening was real! I thought, *How can we let the oldest living oak tree in North America be cut down?* The solution to this problem came in the form of a land trust. The Low Country Open Land Trust now owns the property, while Charleston County Parks and Recreation manage the Angel Oak. The tree is safe, and people can visit for free! I hope you enjoy the story.

The acorn lay on the shore of the beach among the wave-washed clamshells. It looked misplaced among the washed-up seaweed and broken conch shells. As it lay on its sandy bed, instinct told the acorn that this was not the right place for it to bury itself and begin the ritual of life. As these thoughts rushed through its mind, a seagull swooped down from the cloudless sky and began circling overhead.

At first, the circling seagull paid the acorn no attention. As the seagull flew closer to the shore, its piercing eyes spied the acorn. Giving a loud screech, the gull landed close by the acorn and waddled over to investigate.

Surrounded now by dying seaweed, which had been washed ashore from deep ocean currents, the acorn hoped that it was hidden.

The seagull poked its bill among scattered shells, searching for the object it had seen from its view in the sky. Thankfully, lodged between a clump of seaweed and an extra-large cockleshell, the acorn was not visible.

Waves of the rising ocean tide came closer and closer to the hidden acorn and the searching seagull. With each wave, the acorn was in more danger. The salty arms of the ocean would wash away the objects that were keeping the acorn safe. If it was swept out to sea by the waves, the acorn might survive. If it was revealed, the acorn would be the seagull's midday meal.

As the acorn tasted the saltiness of the waves and felt the cockleshell shift in the moving sand, the searching bill of the seagull brushed against the acorn's outer shell. The next instant, the upper and lower sections of the gull's bill crushed tightly down on the acorn. With a flurry of flapping wings and screeches of success, the seagull rose into the air with its prize.

Just as the acorn lost all hope, it suddenly began to fall from the grasp of the seagull. What had startled the seagull enough to make it release its catch?

As gentle fingers lifted the acorn, the acorn could see the gull. With its wings flapping angrily and loudly, the seagull flew away from the visitor, screeching complaints. It paused to give a final look at the acorn and then flew toward out over the breaking waves of the ocean.

The face that greeted the acorn was youthful in its beauty but aged in its texture. The hand that held it was gentle, and the voice was kind yet hoarse and shaky from years of use.

"Well, what do we have here?" asked the voice in its native tongue, Muskogean. "That seagull was just a little too close." With those words, an old woman placed the acorn into a dry, worn pouch made of raccoon skin that smelled of peppermint. The smell of the pouch was comforting to the acorn. The warmth inside wrapped it in a blanket of security, and in its exhaustion, the acorn drifted off to sleep.

The woman was a Kiawah Indian named Hatokwassi, which means dragonfly. She gently patted the pocket where she had placed the acorn. Her warm brown eyes squinted in the bright sunlight as she looked out over the beauty of the ocean. The turbulent winds from the approaching tropical storm had strewn the beach with palm branches and other decay. The acorn, snatched from the safety of an oak tree, had landed on the shore during the night.

Hatokwassi turned to make her way home with her treasures. The departing storm had left not only the acorn but also an assortment of beautiful shells and marine life. She adjusted her basket of clams and oysters, checked the starfish, and shifted the weight of another basket full of berries. With a tired but contented sigh, she made her way toward a bank of dome-shaped dunes covered with sea oats. Scouring the beach for useful materials and food was over for the day.

Hatokwassi finally made her way to the backyard of her home. Circular in design, it consisted of bent poles covered with bark from cypress, and moss and clay had been added for further insulation. Near the dwelling was a bountiful garden of corn, pumpkins, beans, and squash. Among the vegetables were herbs of many varieties and flowers, which grew wild along the coastal area. Stooping over to gather tools for digging, she placed the seashells on the outer fringes of the garden, placed the basket woven from grasses native to the area beside the shells, and reached for a digging tool. Hatokwassi looked around, carefully searching for the right place to plant her acorn. Thinking of the joy that would come from this gift, she found the perfect spot. Close behind where her garden grew, not too close to where her grandchildren loved to play, she knelt in a position of prayer. Sitting back on the heels of her moccasins, Hatokwassi reached into her pouch and brought out the acorn. The prayer she spoke went like this:

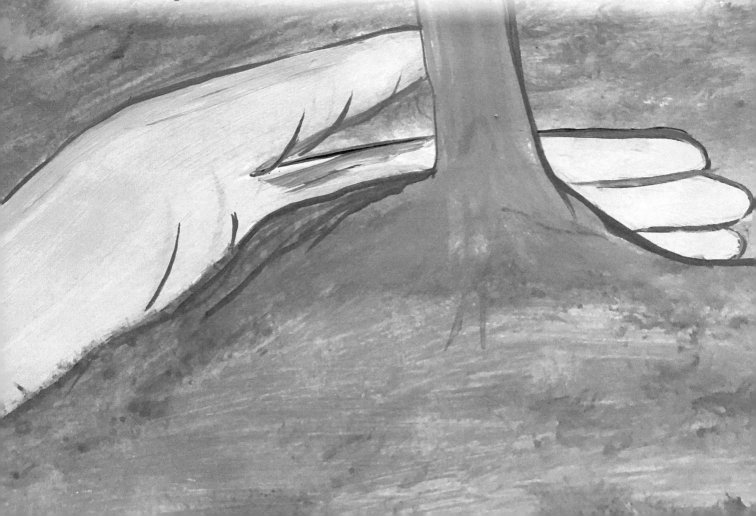

"Strong spirit of the acorn, I accept you as a gift for my village. Your bountiful branches will shade the garden from sun that is too hot, your strong boughs will provide safe arms for the playing of our children, and your plentiful seeds will provide food for the squirrels. May Kiawah, animal, and tree live in harmony. I pray for you to grow and become a mighty oak tree."

Carefully, she placed the acorn into the soil and covered it very gently with a blanket of warm soil. Using water she collected daily from a nearby stream, the old Kiawah sprinkled the covered acorn with water.

Every day, Hatokwassi talked aloud as she enjoyed the bounty of the garden. As she and the other women worked to gather food for their families, nature and native were at peace. Each day before leaving the garden, she spoke directly to the acorn and provided it a generous drink of water.

Soon the acorn awoke to the feel of warmth and moisture. Where was the peppermint-smelling pocket? For some reason, the acorn was not afraid and instead felt very comfortable in this dark, damp new home. The acorn stretched and stretched. Never had it felt so alive! The prayers of Hatokwassi had been heard, and the acorn's cycle of life began. The hard shell coat it wore burst, and the acorn began pushing and thrusting upward toward the warmer outer layer of soil.

It did not take many days before the seedling burst through the soil and found the brightness of the sunlight. Now it could see the beauty within the garden. The warm sunlight and the gentle ocean breeze tickled the emerging sapling. That afternoon, Hatokwassi was delighted to see the changes in the acorn. The old woman greeted it in its new form. The children of the village eagerly welcomed this new creation. They joined hands and sang of its beauty.

The bright sunlight, the spaciousness of its new home, and an adequate water supply enabled the seedling to grow stronger and taller until one day it stood many feet into the sky. From where its roots firmly supported its trunk, the oak tree spread its massive branches toward the heavens. The birds that rested within its canopy had a view of the sandy shoreline of the ocean. This shoreline was the same yet different from the time of Hatokwassi. Though it was the same location where the winds first took the little acorn from its home in a different oak tree, the distance from the river to the ocean was much less. Now the smell of the ocean's saltiness blew faintly over an overgrown garden. As the ocean breeze drifted among the hidden artifacts and tickled the branches of the oak tree, it heard distant sounds of running underneath. The sounds of the Kiawah children who once played beneath this oak tree again filled the air; the great-great-grandchildren of Hatokwassi played their many games beneath its massive branches, echoing from the past. A new century was near.

Time and the tree watched the land pass from the hands of the Kiawah into the hands of strangers. These people worshipped different spirits, and they did not understand the ways of the Indian. In the year 1717, Abraham Waight received the land on which this southern oak stood as part of a small land grant. For four generations, Abraham's descendants enjoyed the bountiful shade of the massive oak. Laughter once again resounded beneath the heavy branches.

Many years later, ownership of the land beneath the oak tree's roots again changed hands. In celebration of a new marriage between Justus and Martha Angel, blessings poured freely. Justus and Martha were proud of the land they had been given. Martha knew of the legend of Hatokwassi and the acorn from the beach. She knew the importance of humanity's balance with nature. Each day Martha filled bird feeders that hung from the branches of what she knew to be the blessed oak. Time slowly moved on, and the tree continued to grow. It was now called Angel Oak.

Four generations of Angel descendants guarded and lived near Angel Oak. The bobwhite quail, the threatened Florida scrub jay, wood ducks, yellow-bellied sapsuckers, wild turkeys, black bears, squirrels, and white-tailed deer benefited from the bounty of its acorns. They ate of the oil that long ago had been so dear to the Kiawah.

Thousands of years later, in the present day, the tree has changed hands once more. The city of Charleston now owns Angel Oak. Many visitors walk underneath the heavy limbs of this magnificent southern oak, which stands in an obscure wooded area of John's Island, South Carolina, some twelve miles beyond the Ashley River. South Carolina historians and preservationists protect the Angel Oak. Tourists from across the country walk its perimeter, photograph its beauty and bounty, and leave amazed at its size. Angel Oak now stands about 65 feet (20 meters) high, with a canopy providing 17,000 square feet (1,600 square meters) of shade. It is 2.47 meters in diameter, and its longest branch spreads out over 27 meters. Some of its branches are so heavy that they have dropped underground for a few feet and then come back up toward the heavens and lay above the ground.

More than fourteen hundred years ago, this tree began its cycle of life. Though no family currently lives beneath its protective boughs, this tree has continued to provide shelter for nesting animals and food for many deer, squirrels, and birds that live in the surrounding woods. Angel Oak has survived countless hurricanes, floods, and earthquakes. Damaged severely by Hurricane Hugo in 1989, it has since recovered. The only threat to Angel Oak comes in the form of human interference. Though surrounding gated fences prevent vandalism of any kind, nearby development of land threatens its existence. The prayer whispered so reverently so many years ago as the oak tree began the ritual of life was answered. Its bountiful branches shaded gardens, its boughs provided a safe playground for many children, and its fruit fed many of nature's creatures. Will harmony between nature and humankind allow the legend of Angel Oak to continue?

Glossary of Terms

acorn: The hard fruit of an oak tree, consisting of a smooth single-seeded nut that is set in a cup-shaped base and ripens from green to brown.

Angel Oak: A live oak that is a native species found throughout the Low Country (coastal South Carolina). It is believed to be in excess of fifteen hundred years old. Its massive, draping limbs and wide-spreading canopy present the aura of an angel, but the tree's name was acquired from its previous owners, Martha and Justin Angel.

artifact: An object made by a human being (e.g., a tool or ornament), especially one that has archaeological or cultural interest.

assortment: A collection of various kinds.

bough: A large main branch of a tree, from which smaller branches grow.

bounty: A plentiful or generous supply.

canopy: The uppermost layer of vegetation in a forest, consisting of the tops of trees forming a kind of ceiling.

century: A period of one hundred years.

circular: Having the shape of a perfect circle, or resembling a circle in shape.

clay: A fine-grained material that occurs naturally in soil and sedimentary rock. It is used in making bricks, ceramics, and cement.

clump: A group of things.

cockleshell: A small rounded or heart-shaped ridged shell in two parts.

conch shell: A spiral shell that may bear long projections and have a flared lip. Tropical marine mollusks live inside.

cypress: A coniferous evergreen tree with dark-green leaves resembling scales.

dune: A mound or ridge of sand formed by wind or water action, typically seen on coasts.

earthquake: A violent shaking of the earth's crust that may cause destruction to buildings and results from the sudden release of tectonic stress along a fault line or from volcanic activity.

emerging: Starting to appear, arise, occur, or develop.

flood: A very large amount of water that has overflowed from a source such as a river or a broken pipe onto a previously dry area.

fringes: The outer edges.

flurry: Burst of activity.

generation: The period of time that it takes for people, animals, or plants to grow up and produce their own offspring; in humans this is held to be between thirty and thirty-five years.

harmony: A situation in which there is friendly agreement or accord.

herbs: Low-growing aromatic plants used fresh or dried for seasoning, for their medicinal properties, or in perfumes. Sage and rosemary are herbs.

hurricane: A severe tropical storm with torrential rain and extremely strong winds. Hurricanes originate in areas of low pressure in equatorial regions of the Atlantic or Caribbean and then strengthen, traveling northwest, north, or northeast.

investigate: To take a look or go and see what has happened.

interference: Something that prevents a natural or desired outcome.

Kiawah: Native American tribe of South Carolina.

legend: A story that has been passed down for generations, especially one that is presented as history but is unlikely to be true.

lodged: To become jammed somewhere.

massive: Extremely large.

misplaced: In a wrong place or position.

moccasin: A Native North American heelless shoe made of deerskin or other soft leather wrapped around the foot and stitched on top.

moss: A simple nonflowering plant that has short stems with small leaves arranged in spirals and resembling scales, and inhabits moist shady sites.

Muskogean: A Hokan-Siouan branch of languages, including Chickasaw, Choctaw, and Creek.

native tongue: The first language that somebody learns to speak.

obscure: Not able to be seen or heard distinctly.

peppermint: A plant of the mint family whose dark-green downy leaves yield peppermint.

piercing: Having an unpleasantly intense quality.

pouch: A small bag or container made of a soft material.

raccoon: A small animal with grayish-black fur, black patches around the eyes, and a long, bushy ringed tail. Native to forests of North and Central America.

ritual: Cycle.

sapling: A young tree with a slender trunk.

scouring: To search something thoroughly and quickly for somebody or something.

screech: A high-pitched grating cry or scream.

sea oats: A protected grass that grows along the eastern coastline and Gulf of Mexico and helps keep the sand and soil from washing away.

seaweed: A plant that grows in the ocean.

shell coat: Hard, protective outer covering.

shift: To move somebody or something to a different position or be moved to a different position.

village: A group of houses and other buildings in a rural area, smaller than a town.

waddled: A way of walking, taking short steps with the body tilting slightly from one side to the other with each step.

woven: Created by weaving.

Bibliography

Angel Oak. https://www.angeloaktree.com/

Cusabo Indians. http://www.sciway.net/hist/indians/cusabo.html

Drake, John C., Associated Press. "Historians Track Hurricanes Back to 1700s." *Live Science*. 27 October 2005. 20 September 2008. http://www.livescience.com/environmenta/ap_051027_hurricane_history.html.

Teacher's Guide text

Here are some ways to enrich the reading of *One Acorn's Journey*. Please feel free to use them in any order and to pick and choose what works for you.

Activate Prior Knowledge

Talk to your class about the life cycle of a tree. Brainstorm the steps in the cycle, find the appropriate vocabulary to identify and draw a diagram based on the classes' understanding. This diagram will be added to after reading the book.

Read the Book Aloud

(Prepare an Anchor Chart for the book where you will add questions from students before and after reading).

(Give students sticky notes). Before you begin reading, do a picture walk through the book. Allow students to ask questions, make comments, and identify the life cycle of the tree when applicable. Encourage them to write their questions on the sticky notes and place them on the Book Anchor Chart. The purpose of this is to remind students that oftentimes our questions are answered in the book.

Read the book, pausing to enjoy the photographs and their relation to the text. Ask students how the pictures help them to understand what is written.

After Reading the Book

Allow students to discuss the book and what emotions the book evoked in them.

What is the author's purpose in writing, *One Acorn's Journey: The Legend of the Angel Oak*? Does the author show bias?

Allow students to revisit their questions on the anchor chart. Answered questions can be removed. Add any further question that students might still have.

Don't forget to go back to your anchor chart and complete any details.

Writing Opportunity

What is a legend? Compare *One Acorn's Journey: The Legend of the Angel Oak* with the definition of a legend. How does it compare?

Students may create a legend of their own.

Environmental/Conservation Study

Encourage students to research and identify local icons. After research, students can prepare posters to promote protection of this local icon and come up with solutions to solve any problems associated with that icon.

Write letters to proper local agencies advocating the protection of said icon.

Feel free to share your experiences: rhondasedwards@gmail.com

About the Author

Raised in southeastern North Carolina, Rhonda has lived in the Low country of South Carolina since 1980. She married her high school sweetheart more than forty years ago and together they have a son and a grandchild.

Rhonda was a stay-at-home mom until her son began school. She then became active in PTA and as a substitute teacher. Encouraged by her husband, Rhonda completed her undergraduate work at the College of Charleston in Charleston, SC, where she graduated with a BS in Elementary Education in 1994. Rhonda then went on to receive her National Board certification as a Middle Childhood Generalist and received her MA in English from a joint program with The College of Charleston and the Citadel in 2005.

Rhonda teaches fourth grade GATE in North Charleston, SC. She was also an adjunct professor for the English Department at Trident Technical College. Edwards is a Fellow of the Charleston Area Writing Project (CAWP), having received this honor the summer of 1994. Being a part of the writing project was one of the best summers Rhonda ever spent. She was able to nurture her love for writing among a supportive encouraging group of fellow teachers/writers.

Living on forty acres with her family, Rhonda enjoys gardening and getting to know the many animals on the homestead. She raises chickens, goats, and ducks along with her two dogs. Rhonda's hobbies include walking the shoreline, searching for shells, looking and checking on loggerhead turtle nests, and enjoying the calming beauty of the ocean.

Printed in the United States
by Baker & Taylor Publisher Services